Walter J. McDonald

Reader's Guide

to

Achieving Excellence in Dealer/Distributor Performance

Walter J. McDonald

Walter J. McDonald

Copyright © 2018, The McDonald Group, Inc. All rights reserved. This book, or parts thereof, may not be reproduced in any form without permission from the publisher. Exceptions are made for brief excerpts used in published reviews. All rights reserved.

Published by The McDonald Group, Inc.
P.O. Box 730, Arlington Heights, IL 60006 USA
www.mcdonaldgroupinc.com

This publication is designed to provide accurate and authoritative information in regard to the subject matter covered. It is sold with the understanding that neither the author nor publisher is engaged in rendering legal, accounting, tax or other professional service. If legal or financial advice or other expert assistance is required, the services of a competent professional person should be sought.

From a Declaration of Principles Jointly Adopted by a Committee of the American Bar Association and a Committee of Publishers and Associations.

Because of the dynamic nature of the Internet,
any web address or links contained in this book
may have changed since publication and may no longer be valid.

ISBN 1986436322

ISBN-13: 9781986436328

READER's GUIDE to *Achieving Excellence in Dealer/Distributor Performance*

The Master's Program in Dealer Management
By Walter J. McDonald

Achieving Excellence in Dealer/Distributor Performance

★   <u>Also</u>:   Reader's Guide to *Achieving Excellence in Dealer/Distributor Performance*

Strategies, Tactics, Operations for Achieving Dealer Excellence

★   <u>Also</u>:   Reader's Guide to *Strategies, Tactics, Operations for Achieving Excellence*

Dealer Problem Solving Handbook

Workbook and Study Guide for the Master's Program in Dealer Management

A complete description of each volume is contained on www.mcdonaldgroupinc.com.
Discounts for quantity orders of this text as well as other volumes in Walter McDonald's six-volume set are available.
Please contact the author at *Walt@mcdonaldgroupinc.com.*

Walter J. McDonald

DEDICATION

My gratitude to the industry leaders who have purchased my books, utilized them in their businesses and recommended them to their friends and associates.

Walter J. McDonald

CONTENTS

Acknowledgments	1
Introduction	2
How to Use This Book	3
Where to Begin—Identify Current Primary Concerns	4
Let's Get Started	5
Bus Drivers, Controls, Maps and Tools	8
Critical Profit Variables	9
Managing the Dealership Overall	10
Managing Parts Operations	11
Managing Service Operations	12
Managing Rentals and Used Equipment Operations	13
Managing New Equipment Operations	16
Managing Customer Training and Customer Retention	18
Aftermarket Management	19
Machinery Sales Management	20
Ultimate Survival	21
A Few More Words from The Coach	22
SPECIAL REPORT #1—Jim Wilson How Dealers Can Avoid Problems with OEM Sales and Service Agreements: Are They Functional or Fractured?	24
SPECIAL REPORT #2—Chris Shields 8TH Year Dealer Progress Review of 2010 McDonald Product Support Management Workshop	33
The Master's Program in Dealer Management **Books**	39
The Master's Program in Dealer Management **Workshop**	41
Executive Sales and Sales Management **Workshop**	44
About the Author	49
Free Articles from The McDonald Group, Inc.	50

Walter J. McDonald

ACKNOWLEDGMENTS

Thank you to the thousands of dealer managers and executives who have provided insight into how to solve the problems faced by machinery and equipment dealerships all over the planet.

This *Reader's Guide* is designed to assist…

>Dealer/distributor owners, investors, managers, supervisors and sons/daughters of bosses.

>Manufacturer executives, sales and aftermarket managers and young managers on the way up.

>Banks, investors, lenders and financial institutions.

>In these industries…
>>Construction Equipment
>>Forklift
>>Heavy Duty Truck
>>Fire Apparatus
>>Emergency Vehicles
>>Materials Handling
>>AG Machinery
>>Pump and Generator
>>Industrial Machinery and Equipment
>>Municipal Equipment
>>Mining Machinery
>>GPS Telematics
>>Turf Management

Walter J. McDonald

INTRODUCTION

This *Reader's Guide* provides the background story on how the content of my many workshops along with the collective collaboration of world class dealers can help you become more successful.

What is a *Reader's Guide?* This *Reader's Guide,* created by the Author, delivers a practical introduction to *Achieving Excellence in Dealer/Distributor Performance,* guiding readers towards a thorough understanding of the text. You will gain insights as to why each section is important. This *Guide* pinpoints and highlights areas that could be especially valuable to you in your dealer business. I detail what actions you can take to gain and maintain significant competitive advantage.

Please keep in mind, at 377 pages, *Achieving Excellence in Dealer/Distributor Performance* is a very comprehensive text. So, please take your time. I suggest you read one section and then reflect on the management tools and best practices presented. Use post-it notes to mark pages you would like to discuss with me. I would welcome your questions and comments:

walt@mcdonaldgroupinc.com

We also have a handy color bookmark available for the asking with a Remedial Action Project Summary Listing on the reverse side. This is a convenient place to note problems, opportunities or issues for further review. Simply email me your physical address with postal code and I will mail you a free one.

READER's GUIDE to *Achieving Excellence in Dealer/Distributor Performance*

HOW TO USE THIS *Reader's Guide*

As discussed in *Achieving Excellence in Dealer/Distributor Performance,* there are six steps for a successful dealer/distributor *Operations Improvement Program.*

1. Identify and study world-class machinery dealer quantitative operations performance achievements.

2. Measure your current company performance against High-Performance Benchmarks.

3. Determine "gaps," differences between your current Performance and World Class Dealer Benchmarks.

4. Rank performance deficiencies by financial impact and priority. (Where can you really leverage your effort?)

5. Structure remedial Action Plans to correct and work toward eliminating priority performance deficiencies.

6. Energize your company management team into a continuous improvement program.

As you work your way through your copy of *Achieving Excellence in Dealer/Distributor Performance,* you will find suggested approaches and guidelines for each of these steps. The book page margins are extra wide to give you room for notes as you study the text.

Walter J. McDonald

WHERE TO BEGIN-Identify Current Primary Concerns

Before you read the *Achieving Excellence* text, I suggest you begin by giving some thought to your overall business. List your primary concerns for each area below. State your issues in terms of questions such as *How do we improve our overall parts fill rate to the service department?* Or, *How do we increase our rental utilization?* Or, *Why are we so cash poor?*

How do we...

   In the Parts Department:

   In the Service Department:

   In the Rental Department:

   In New Machinery Sales:

   In Used Machinery Sales:

   In Administration and Finance:

This little exercise could help you clarify what areas are giving you the most concern before you begin. As you read through *Achieving Excellence,* update your list of "Hot Topics" with "how to" answers.

If you need assistance defining your problems or structuring solutions, email me for help: walt@mcdonaldgroupinc.com.

READER's GUIDE to *Achieving Excellence in Dealer/Distributor Performance*

LET'S GET STARTED

Read the beginning of *Achieving Excellence*, through p. 10.
> As you look over the broad content in the *Table of Contents, List of Figures and Illustrations* and *List of Tables and Data Displays,* you may wish to highlight or check off sections that are of particular interest.

How this Book Can Help, p. 11 – 12
> Depending on your current area of responsibility and primary interest, a suggested approach to the book is offered for you.

A Realistic Look at Your Possible Future, p. 12 – 16.
> If you are quantitatively inclined, this short exercise will help you project your potential for Incremental *Profit after Direct Expense*.

> To simplify the model, your current annual new machine sales volume remains constant. Using the current *Sales Mix* of high performance dealers in your industry, you can project a possible future sales level for Used Machine, Rentals, Parts, Service Labor and Customer Training. This is based on your current new machine sales.

> Next, the projected *Profit after Direct Expense* is calculated for each Revenue Center.

> Then, deduct your Current *Profit after Direct Expense* (Before Corporate Overhead Allocation).

The result is your **Big Courageous Profit Potential**. And, this Incremental Profit target is based on what other successful dealers are doing in your industry.

This is the process...

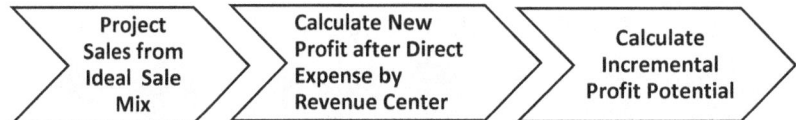

This **exercise** helps you estimate a possible financial future at optimum profitability based on achievements of high performance dealers.

This **assessment** demonstrates the value of improving overall dealer sales mix based on your current new machinery sales volume. The objective is not to decrease machine sales, but to increase service, parts and rentals.

This **projection** is based on the optimum Sales Mix for high-performance dealers in your industry *p.66*. Please contact me if you would like help with this analysis.

Preface, Prologue, A CPA's Financial Perspective, p. 17 – 27.

Tim Hilton represents the Material Handling Industry. Nick McGaughey reflects dealer financial management. John Vandy represents Construction Machinery.

READER's GUIDE to *Achieving Excellence in Dealer/Distributor Performance*

Introduction, How Book Is Organized, Terminology, p. 28-31.

> The Introduction helps explain how this book can help you increase *Business Enterprise Value. How This Book Is Organized* provides an overview of the entire work. *Terminology* helps builds a common vocabulary.

Acknowledgements, p. 32 – 34.

> Undeniably, *Achieving Excellence* would never have been possible without the support of many industry leaders, who, for many years, worked diligently, establishing World-Class Best Practices and Performance Benchmarks.

Importance of Quants, p. 35 – 38.

> If you can't measure it, you will never manage it! As described in these pages, only five elements drive World Class dealer performance.

> Proper achievement of each management task will help ensure successful navigation through economic ups and downs. Perhaps, the most critical of these tasks, is the proper use of competitive analytics: How you can get ahead and make certain you are staying ahead!

Chapter 1

in *Achieving Excellence in Dealer/Distributor Performance*

BUS DRIVERS, CONTROLS, MAPS and TOOLS, P. 40

As we gain insight into "The Big Picture" in this Chapter, there appear to be six primary obstacles preventing many dealer principals from taking their business to where they want to go. We will examine each of these obstacles in detail.

As you continue to broaden your management education, I strongly recommend the following texts for great insights:

According to Jim Collins in *Good to Great,* the first step in moving your bus from here to there is not <u>where</u> you are going, but <u>who</u> is going to be on the bus to help you get there. These Revenue Center *Bus Drivers* (business leaders) are critical to your success.

This <u>who</u> issue is further examined by Gino Wickman in his very provocative book, *Traction: Get a Grip on Your Business.*

Gino Wickman's *Traction* is an exceptional book for dealers who want to grow. He helps you analyze and think about the six components of your business: Vision, People, Data, Issues, Process and Traction. I highly recommend it.

Another obstacle to growth is often getting crucial projects completed. Sean Covey's *The 4 Disciplines of Execution* is an exceptionally well written guide for dealer management teams on how to set and achieve extraordinary goals, how effective execution is achieved.

READER's GUIDE to *Achieving Excellence in Dealer/Distributor Performance*

Chapter 2

CRITICAL PROFIT VARIABLES – P. 45

The second insight we will use to help understand *The Big Picture* in Dealer Development is my Executive Summary of the 48 Critical Profit Variables (CPV). This can serve as a useful coaching tool for your newer managers. I provide a clear definition and explanation for each CPV.

Quantitative Performance Benchmarks are your *Critical Profit Variables*. These are the variables you can change that have great impact on your business. These definitions provide an important common vocabulary for your management team.

Note: Throughout the text are highlighted sidebars that include Hot Tips and Best Management Practices. On *page 63*, for example, is a comprehensive, but inexpensive recommended self-study DVD management education kit from TheGreatCourses.com.

Chapter 3

MANAGING THE DEALERSHIP OVERALL, P. 66

Detailed definitions for the 48 Critical Profit Variables (quantitative performance goals) for Dealer Revenue Centers begin here: Overall Dealer Performance, Parts, Service, Rentals (Hires), New and Used Machinery and Customer Training.

World-class dealer scores are illustrated for comparisons to your current operations. Remember, these 48 "world class" performance levels should be considered _directional_. It doesn't matter what your score is today. There are no good or bad scores. However, if your score is substantially below the performance benchmark goal, you have significant opportunity for improvement. These are most likely the best places to start in your overall profit improvement plan.

Pay close attention to
- #1) *Sales Mix p. 66,* *
- #2) *Absorption Rate p. 68,*
- #4) *Gross Profit Margin p. 70* and
- #6) *Profit After Direct Expenses* (PADE) *p. 73.*

#9) The *Growth Potential Index p. 75,* helps you calculate the maximum total annual sales increase you can support with your current cash generating capability. Your *Growth Potential Index* can be increased by improving gross profit margin or reducing overall expenses. Start looking in Service Labor for margin improvement opportunities, your best untapped source.

*/ Critical Profit Variables #1) to #48), pages 66 - 129.

READER's GUIDE to *Achieving Excellence in Dealer/Distributor Performance*

Chapter 4

MANAGING PARTS OPERATIONS, P. 77

#10) *Percent of Available Business p. 77,* is one of the most useful metrics to project parts market potential and your current parts market share. The calculation is based on your product line unit population. This dynamite, easy-to-use marketing tool is further explained in Chapter 10, *16 Tools to Build Service Business p. 146.*

Your most critical performance indicator is #11) *Off-Shelf Parts Fill Rate to Service p. 79.* Yet, many dealers still do not measure it. If your technician does not have a needed part, this problem often cascades into significant dealer management heart burn, customer outrage and serious intramural conflict.

If your annual parts sales volume is over US$7 million, pay close attention to *Investigate Strategic Pricing, p. 86.* Incremental bottom line margin increases of 2 to 4 points are being achieved today in several dealer parts departments through use of this tool.

Chapter 5

MANAGING SERVICE OPERATIONS, P. 89

The Big Three Service Management challenges are:

a.   Projection of service labor market potential.

b.   Selling service labor at or above high-profit dealer benchmark margins.

c.   Managing labor quality and productivity.

Chapter 4, *p. 77* and Chapter 5, *p. 89* examine "Performance Benchmarks" in *Parts and Service*. Focus is on what must be done to accelerate aftermarket market share growth and profitability.

Of particular importance and value is the concept of measuring parts and labor Sales Potential by Product Category and projecting your market share "Percent of Available Business" (PAB). These concepts are illustrated on p. 78 and on p. 149.

The bottom line is that customers who are under PM (Planned Maintenance) contracts with your dealership will spend 7 times more with you than an identical customers not under a PM agreement.

And, you will see over and over again that the secret to improving profitable aftermarket parts and service sales is through machinery and equipment inspections <u>if properly conducted</u> during the PM procedure.

Chapter 6

MANAGING RENTALS AND USED EQUIPMENT OPERATIONS, P. 104

RENTALS

Once you and your financial advisors have properly structured the ownership and financing model* for your rental (hire) fleet, it's time to look at Rental Operations.

The three issues that seem to cause the most problems for dealers in my Rental Management Workshop are related to *Utilization*, *Maintenance Cost Control* and *Margins*.

Both *Time and Dollar Utilization* should be measured by product category as outlined in Benchmark (#33) *p.104*. Just monitoring time utilization can easily cover up margin, discounting and profitability problems.

Rental Maintenance Cost Control (#34) *p. 106,* requires close collaboration between sales, rentals and service.

If Rental Maintenance is too high, conduct a continuous "why" investigation until the primary cause is identified.

Unfortunately, few dealers actually calculate their *Rental Rates Based on Cost and Gross Profit Margin Objective* (#37) *p. 108*.

*/ For helpful guidelines on how to structure rental assets, cost structure and proper recognition of rental revenue see my dealer management text, *Strategies, Tactics, Operations for Achieving Dealer Excellence,* pages 274 – 277.

The impact of poor pricing and margin contribution is illustrated in Table 8, *Rental Return on Investment* p. 107. This table compares impact of 6% rental revenue per month as percentage of overall fleet acquisition cost with a much lower 3.6% and the resulting lower rental revenue.

USED EQUIPMENT

The most important two issues in *Used Machinery Management* are

a) Used machine turnover (#38) *p. 111* and,

b) Proper establishment of purchase price for used unit from customer *p. 116*.

Fig. 14 *p. 116*, illustrates the importance of establishing wholesale value for the potential trade. What can you get for it in cash, within 48 hours, from another dealer? This is *wholesale value*.

The customer is responsible for maintenance during the time he owns the unit. Therefore, the accurate cost estimate of required repairs to bring the unit up to sellable condition must be deducted from wholesale value to determine <u>purchase price from the customer</u>.

CRUCIAL POINT: The <u>dealer selling price</u> for the unit is developed by adding desired margin to the <u>wholesale value</u>.

Fig. 16 *p. 118* shows results of an OEM's used equipment trading analysis study of dealer transactions. By examining many used equipment sales, it was confirmed that the longer the unit remains in dealer inventory, the lower the margin at time of sale. Highest margins were often on used units pre-sold to another customer before the trade. Break even on margins appears at the 90 day period. Hence, the Axiom, "90 and out!"

If you have over 25 – 30 used equipment units, consider the Over/Under Report shown in Table 9 *p. 113*. You want to make certain you are never "upside down" in your fleet. This occurs when book value of your inventory is higher than cash wholesale market value. If the economy softens, used equipment values could rapidly deteriorate and you could be in trouble. Declining used equipment values is one of the leading indicators of a softening economy.

Chapter 7

MANAGING NEW EQUIPMENT OPERATIONS, P. 121

Clearly, the two big Sales Management issues are unit volume and gross profit margin. And, two big obstacles are #43) *Deal Visibility Rate p. 124* and, #44) *Deal Closure Rate p.125*.

If your field sales rep participates in or only "sees" 20% of the deals in the territory, market share and margin improvements are nearly impossible to attain. With few deals in his/her sales pipeline, there is tremendous pressure to close what little is there.

You often hear a variation on "Give me the lowest price and I'll really show you some salesmanship!" (The two sets of selling skills essential to strengthen *Visibility Rate* and *Closure Rate* are detailed in Chapter 25, *p. 267*, *Photo Shoot on the Serengeti.*

A large contributor to the problem is low Daily Sales Territory Coverage Intensity (#45) *p. 127*. If your new sales rep launch procedure does not get them up to satisfactory coverage performance within the first 90 days, three more years of bad habits are going to be very difficult to change. (See *Strategies, Tactics, Operations for Achieving Dealer Excellence,* Chapter 18, pages 459 – 510, *"Accelerated Start-Up, How to get your brand new sales rep productive in 90 days."* This is a dynamite program was written in blood with experience sales managers.)

You want your reps to work smarter and harder. Chapter 20 *p. 232, Achieving 5 Star Sales Management* offers several tools on how you can help your sales reps work more effectively.

READER's GUIDE to *Achieving Excellence in Dealer/Distributor Performance*

An important Sales Management metric is #41) *p. 122, Return on Sales Compensation Investment by Sales Rep.* Is your candidate paying his/her way? This tool can easily help you spot problems, month by month.

If you are having problems in this area, study Chapter 27 *p. 282, Are You Ready to Increase Your Competitiveness?* I have found Figure 36 *p. 288, Performance Appraisal Logic* extremely helpful over the years, as I worked on performance development issues with sales reps on my team.

Finally, for your sales personnel, the two "Best Practices" self-appraisals on *p. 262* through *p. 274* are very useful. "Sales Rep Confidential: Are You a Dinosaur?" is followed by "Photo Shoot on the Serengeti, How to Improve Deal Visibility, Closure Rate."

Chapter 8

MANAGING CUSTOMER TRAINING AND CUSTOMER RETENTION, P. 130

An exciting new emerging Revenue Center is *Customer Training* which includes operator training. If managed properly, this Revenue Center can generate *Profit after Direct Expense* of at least 40% (#47) *p. 131.* And, several dealers are working toward achieving at least 1% of total dealer sales in customer training sales (#46) *p. 130.*

#48), p. 131, *Year Over Year Customer Retention Rate* is the easiest and best way to monitor your Annual Customer Retention Rate. Customer attrition happens, but you should maintain active relationships with <u>at least</u> 85% of your accounts from year to year.

If your Customer Retention Rate is below 85%, it is probably only one of many clues indicating you are having big problems.

(A highly useful emergency procedure to help reduce customer defections and turnover is "The Customer Round Table." See *Strategies Tactics, Operations for Achieving Dealer Excellence,* pages 211 – 212. It really work well. It can also be used if you have just acquired a new territory for your Area of Responsibility (AOR) and need to immediately detect the big, current customer issues.)

READER's GUIDE to *Achieving Excellence in Dealer/Distributor Performance*

Chapters 9 - 17

AFTERMARKET MANAGEMENT, P. 133

In many dealerships, the dealer product support team does much of the work. But, unfortunately, this team often only receives a paltry amount of recognition.

Three trends have developed that are encouraging:

1. New machinery sales teams are beginning to recognize the enormous advantages a dealership can gain by positioning product support as a competitive weapon. You can start by including the product support executive on the sales presentation team, especially on large, multi-unit deals.

2. We are now seeing more CEO-COO appointments from the product support leadership ranks.

3. Because of finally recognizing the impact of product support on *Absorption Rate*, owners are more eager today to make investments in aftermarket than ever before.

This portfolio of aftermarket management articles represent much of my work on behalf of my clients in the aftermarket.

Note: Please See SPECIAL REPORT #2, p. 33 in this Reader's Guide By Chris Shields, V.P. Product Support at Hugg & Hall on his 8-year successful Aftermarket Development efforts.

Chapters **18 – 27**

MACHINERY SALES MANAGEMENT, P. 217

In an environment of intense competitive pressure and often dwindling OEM support, my clients on the sales team need all the help they can get. This portfolio of articles in Chapters 18 – 27, for machinery sales management focuses on three areas:

1. Strengthening sales management skills.

2. Removing obstacles to higher new machine margins.

3. Highlighting selling skills essential to increasing market share and deal profitability.

Of particular value is my *Dealer Executive Sales Management and Executive Selling Skills Workshop.* I will customize selling case studies for your dealership with your products in your markets against your current competitors. See pages 44 – 48 that follow in this Reader's Guide.

READER's GUIDE to *Achieving Excellence in Dealer/Distributor Performance*

Chapters 28 – 30

ULTIMATE SURVIVAL, Page 289

Here we examine dealer financial health and relationships between dealers and their manufacturer(s). Suggestions are offered on how to secure closer, more positive OEM partnerships. And, we look at cash management.

Both issues are related to your *Ultimate Survival!*

Chapter 30 *p. 309* is essential reading to help ensure optimum positive cash flow.

28. How Customers Evaluate a Potential Dealer

29. How Dealers Evaluate their Manufacturer with Trends on How Manufacturers Look at Dealers

30. How to Avoid Death by 10.000 cuts: How to Improve Cash Flow and Velocity.

Please see our related SPECIAL REPORT #1 by Jim Wilson in this *Reader's Guide* on

How Dealers Can Avoid Problems with OEM Sales and Service Agreements

Jim Wilson, Director of Dealer Development, MCFA (ret.) prepared these recommendations based on his many years' experience. This SPECIAL REPORT could be most helpful to your entire senior management team. See pages 24 – 31.

Chapter **30+**

A FEW MORE WORDS FROM THE COACH, Page 322

As your management coach, I encourage you to take action and avoid "paralysis by analysis." Execute! Execute!

CAUTION: It's easy to get bogged down in "paralysis by analysis."

Therefore, I suggest you:

1. Take Action: Grow your top line by at least 2.5% points faster than your local equipment market.
2. Continuously improve your effective service billing rate.
3. Improve your median customer GM% by 3 points.
3. Make more new customer contacts this week over last.

"Action is a great restorer and builder of confidence. Inaction is not only the result, but the cause, of fear." —*Norman Vincent Peale*

NOTE: For really practical additional help, see Sean Covey's new book, *The 4 Disciplines of Execution,* available on Amazon.com.

APPENDIX

My *Master's Program in Dealer Management* p. 366, is the "how to" program on how I can help you and your management team implement the concepts covered in this text in your dealership. This is the high-impact workshop I've conducted with dealer leadership teams all over the world.

Please see SPECIAL REPORT #2 that follows in this Reader's Guide, page 33, on what you can expect from this dynamite dealer management training workshop.

• • • • •

Thank you sincerely for your interest in my work. Please let me know how else I can be of service to you. And, please recommend my texts to your associates.

walt@mcdonaldgroupinc.com

Walter J. McDonald

SPECIAL REPORT #1

How Dealers Can Avoid Problems with OEM Sales and Service Agreements: Are They Functional or Fractured?

> *Note:* This SPECIAL REPORT was prepared by James M. Wilson, Principal Consultant with The McDonald Group. Mr. Wilson brings 42 years' experience with Caterpillar, Inc., and related companies in North and South America, Europe, Africa and the Middle East. He directed Marketing Regions, Advertising and Marketing Programs, Corporate National Accounts and Dealer Development and Relations. He worked internationally in the areas of dealer appointments, best practices, and performance assessments and recognition.
> Mr. Wilson is willing to suggest resources for helping to resolve Sales and Service Agreement disputes.
> (jmwilson0426@gmail.com)

Mr. Wilson's Report:

After almost a 50-year career working in the equipment industry, both for OEMs and as a consultant to dealers/distributors, I'd like to share just a few simple observations. In a worst case scenario these thoughts and recommendations may help you and your OEM get to "yes "rather than battling out legalities in court.

BACKGROUND

When I took my first job as an **OEM** division manager many years ago, my boss said:

> "We don't run our business on Sales and Service Agreements. Look at them for your dealers then put the documents in the drawer. Hopefully, you can leave them there."

What he meant was if both parties want the relationship to work, they don't need to govern their daily business by a *Sales and Service Agreement (Agreement)*. However, both the **OEM** and the dealer, as they conduct their business, need to be respectful and mindful of the intentions, mutual expectations and landscape defined by a business Agreement.

CAUSES OF CONFLICT

When two parties begin to constantly scrimmage over the language of an Agreement in their day-to-day operations, communications and trust have begun to break down and customers may get caught between these clashes. Although not limited to these reasons, here are eight common causes:

1. Both parties misunderstood the Agreement.

2. The wording of the Agreement was ambiguous.

3. Key principals to the Agreement have changed (retirements, promotions, death or, resignations).

4. Uncertainty as to which Agreement is in effect.

5. Lack of familiarity with the Agreement.

6. A sense that conditions have changed over time and the Agreement could be unreasonable.

7. One or both parties never intended to honor the Agreement.

8. State or federal law prohibit certain aspects of an Agreement.

THREE CASES

How easily can things go wrong? In one situation the OEM had gone through a cycle of Agreements due to brand acquisitions and mergers. This OEM lost sight of what particular Agreements dealers were still operating under.

In another case, when a distributor principal retired, his successor neither grasped the Agreement nor sufficiently familiarized himself with it.

And, in a third situation, the dealer principal was a neighbor of the CEO of his OEM in a resort community. The principal leveraged this with his OEM contacts and inferred that he had protection from some aspects of the Agreement. When the CEO retired, this house of cards collapsed and the dealer was replaced for non-performance. The morale of this story is if you are a dealer, do not assume that special relationships exempt you from complying with the letter of an Agreement.

All of these situations resulted in expensive and time consuming litigation that could have been avoided.

RECOMMENDATION—*Ensure Clarity*

Here are some constructive thoughts that some may find helpful.

View the Sales and Service Agreement like you would with some of the new safety features and instruments on modern vehicles. One must become familiar with them. They exist to keep you from running off the road or into someone.

Of course, you can't drive a vehicle by just focusing your eye on the instruments. Nor can you run a business by becoming overwrought over every nuance in a sales and service agreement. However, it is essential in this age of excessive litigation, that an experienced lawyer on contractual Agreements makes sure that the relevant language is as clear and concise as possible and that you understand the obligations.

RECOMMENDATION—*Periodic Agreement Review*

Whether you work for an OEM or a distributor, I recommend your company makes sure key parties subject to the Agreement get a periodic review and training session on the spirit of the document governing their business conduct. If they have questions, then do your best to answer them or get an official interpretation. A once a year review should be sufficient.

RECOMMENDATION—*Annual Compliance Verification*

Likewise, signers to an **Agreement** or their designated representatives should formally meet at least once a year with one another to verify compliance with an **Agreement** and/or satisfaction with the relationship. For the twenty percent of your **Agreements** that feed eighty percent of your business, there is too much at stake not to formalize these processes. Anticipate potential problems and head them off before they exist.

RECOMMENDATION— *Update New Executives on Agreements*

If new people of authority are brought on board such as a dealer principal, general manager, department head, or regional manager, it is highly advisable that not too much time elapses without giving them some exposure to the critical **Agreements** that drive your business. If you fail to do this, one of your people might violate the **Agreement**. In a worse case, this blunder could end the business relationship or result in the offended party's refusal to work with the individual who violated the agreement.

RECOMMENDATION— *OEMs: Keep Agreements Current*

If you are an **OEM**, limit the life of your **Agreements** so that they have meaning and don't become entitlements. This forces you to keep them current and to standardize the language.

RECOMMENDATION— *Recognize Anniversaries*

For the important parties you do business with, whether dealer/distributor or OEM, thank them for doing business with you. On anniversaries ending in five even consider a special dinner or lunch. This is not a celebration of longevity of the Agreement because that may designate entitlement, but rather a nice human touch that says you value the business the other party has given you.

There are just a few reasons why you may have provisions for immediate termination of the Agreement. For example:

- Committing fraud.

- Misrepresentation on a matter material to the agreement.

- Breach of the agreement because of a refusal to do what was agreed upon.

- A change of the principal on the agreement without the approval of the other party.

Everything else should usually be subject to a *cure period*. The "cure period" is part of a formal written warning letter and it sets a deadline to correct a violation of the Agreement and it usually requires a formal written action plan and specific timetable for achievement.

Having to enter into a new Agreement after a defined period of time has value to both parties. It is sort of like repeating your wedding vows. Industry and market dynamics may have changed enough to merit an overhaul of a standard Agreement. An update may also allow for inserting a side letter that recognizes the unique circumstances of an individual relationship.

If you are entering into a first time business relationship, both the **OEM** and distributor/dealer must recognize that newness means that performance goals must be reasonable and not what would be set for an established relationship. If you are a distributor, get in writing what support the **OEM** will provide during a startup period over several months.

WHAT TO DO IF A DISPUTE OCCURS

What do you do when a dispute emerges over the language of the Agreement? How you react may determine whether the business relationship survives.

First, it is important to know if an **OEM** tolerates an omission by a dealer regarding a particular provision, then it may set a precedent that undermines all Agreements regarding that particular provision. So most **OEM**s will push back hard to enforce compliance. They usually have more financial resources than a dealer to defend their Agreements.

If an **OEM** or a distributor sends a warning or *demand letter*, the relationship has begun to spiral toward disaster. A "demand letter" states the provision of an Agreement that has been trespassed and spells out the action or next steps the **OEM** expects. It can range from surrendering the Agreement to requesting a meeting to discuss resolution.

Getting to this state can be avoided by speaking to one another openly and honestly about a perceived offense. This first step may clear up legitimate misunderstandings or even lead to an amendment to the existing Agreement.

Neutral Third Party Review

If an Agreement cannot be resolved through civil discussion and negotiation, then before taking the matter to the courts, you should consider retaining a neutral third party to review your situation and to see if he can guide you to a resolution, short of a lawsuit proving detrimental to both parties.

Arbitration

A next step may be arbitration. This may prove less destructive, expensive, and disruptive to business than subpoenas for files, records, emails, letters, and giving and responding to depositions.

Downside of Litigation

When a relationship has degenerated to litigation, you must assume your customers and employees will get wind of it. Some may leave your business or question your integrity. And, be prepared to pay a high price for ego or ignorance. If you go to court, a final settlement may take years due to appeal processes. This can be a drain on your financial as well as personal and family health.

FINAL THOUGHTS

It is important to stay familiar with the critical language in your Agreement. Be sure you know what you signed when you entered into an Agreement. If you take exception to standard language in an Agreement, try to negotiate for a valid exception before signing it. Then do your best to honor your Agreement, recognizing that there is always room for some legitimate interpretation or at the very least an apology for an offense and corrective action.

If the offended party is open to discussing corrective action or cure period as mentioned earlier, do make sure that your counterpart to the Agreement concurs with the steps, measurements, and timeframes. Then make sure your team understands the stakes and importance of executing the new action plan you proposed to remedy the violation. If your company falls short of the plan, your business may not get another chance to comply with the Agreement.

If for some reason you cannot continue to operate under an existing Agreement, then meet with the other party and work to either amend the Agreement or end the relationship in a manner that is least disruptive to both businesses.

Finally, remember, both distributors and OEMS can acquire a negative reputation in their industry for how they conduct themselves in these matters, possibly making it more difficult to find a future business representative/supplier. You may assume all disputes are confidential, but somehow over time, word has a way of getting around to either the dealer network and/or the industry.

* * *

READER's GUIDE to *Achieving Excellence in Dealer/Distributor Performance*

SPECIAL REPORT #2

8th Year Dealer Progress Review of 2010 McDonald Group, Inc. Product Support Management Workshop

> *Note:* The following SPECIAL REPORT *was prepared by* Chris Shields, Vice President-Product Support, Hugg & Hall Equipment Company. With 13 locations in Arkansas, Louisiana and Oklahoma, selling and supporting over 12 different equipment categories, this highly successful dealership has an incredibly complex Product Support challenge. Mr. Shields sponsored Walter McDonald's 3-day Dealer Management Development Program in 2010 for his entire Product Support Management Team including all Service and Parts Managers, Customer Service Reps and Service Supervisory personnel.

Mr. Shield's Report:

The Product Support Management Training and Development Opportunity:

- *To assemble our entire team of Parts & Service management, in one room, to gain better understanding of what key management measurements for each AOR (Area of Responsibility) should be.*

- *To understand the operating expectations of each department, the differences and their direct correlation with each other.*

- *To achieve deep understanding and gain commitments from each other, that Parts & Service are practically one.*

What We Knew But Didn't Fully Understand:

- 54% of our parts sales are generated through a repair order. Combine those parts sales with total labor revenue generated through a repair order and you arrive at the total contribution of high profit revenue generated through a repair order and a dealers Service Department.

- Our Parts & Service departments were in a constant battle between each other. To be honest, the battle can still rage. It always will when two departments are so reliant on one or the other fulfilling their side of the required work to get all the work done.

- Both were taught well by our coach and instructor, Walter McDonald: *How to execute key processes and carry out expected tasks of their departments.*

We Had Key Measurements for Each Department:

- Parts: Key inventory measures consisted of – Inventory Turns, Inventory Value, Deadstock % of total inventory value.

- Service: Key Inventory Measures consisted of- WIP (Work in Process) Aging, Percent of Labor Dollars closed in last 3 days of a month, Lost Time and Service Re-Work Percent.

However, I believed we lacked real understanding of <u>why</u> we did what we did. What are our real roles in this business and how we might not be looking at all the right things, in the right way?

Connecting the dots:

- The Service Department is the backbone of any highly profitable, customer driven dealership.
- The Parts Department is the ultimate support department of the Service Department.

In that context and taking information directly from Walter's workshop we added focus in the following areas.

Parts: Focus began in 2011 after hiring a Corporate Parts Manager (outcomes below reflect 2014 – 2017 as a result of 2 acquisitions in 2013 that greatly inflated Parts & Service sales against old organization)

- Measuring our off-the-shelf Fill Rate – Beginning in 2011 to date, we have averaged a Fill Rate for stocking items of 93.33% against Walter's performance target of >88-92%.
- Implemented daily inventory cycle counts set to achieve 4 full inventory counts in a year vs. the practice of performing one full inventory count annually.

We have the expectation of < 1% item count variance. Accuracy of on-hand inventory plays a significant role in the accuracy of our system's calculated stock ordering formula. And, accuracy of inventory count in the system is an integral contributor to our off-shelf parts fill rate achievement.

- Moving toward better analysis of the cause and effect of emergency backorders and our efficiency in expediting EBO's (Emergency Back Orders).

Service: Focus began in 2013 after hiring a Corporate Service Manager (outcomes below reflect 2014 – 2017 as a result of 2 acquisitions in 2013 that greatly inflated Parts & Service sales against old organization)

- Measuring Technician Productivity – now associated with individual performance reviews and technician incentive plans.
- Measuring Technician Recovery (Productivity) Rate
- Increase Customer Labor Rate using the customer Labor Rate Multiple equation as a benchmarking tool – benchmark of 2.9-3.3
  1. 2013 - Labor Rate Multiple = 2.89
  2. 2017 - Labor Rate Multiple = 3.52*

Began to measure (AUT) Acceptable Unapplied Time & (UUT) Unacceptable Unapplied Time in hours with goals of =/< 10% & 2.5% of total hours as our tolerances –
1. 2013 – AUT = 13% & UUT = 7%
2. 2017 – AUT = 14%* & UUT = 4%

*First year of "use it or lose it" vacation policy

Outcomes:

- Service Gross Margin (including our discounted internal rate structure)
  2013 – 57%
  2017 – 65%

- Absorption Rate with rental Gross Profit & overall corporate expenses
  2013 – 96%
  2017 – 104%

- Absorption Rate without rental GP & expenses (measure of Parts & Service absorption only)
  2013 – 83%
  2017 – 87%

- Parts Financials: 4 Year Period 2014-2017
  Sales increased 20%
  Gross Profit increased 26%
  Net Income increased 21%

- Service Financials: 4 Year Period 2014-2017
  Sales increased 27%
  Gross Profit increased 42%
  Net Income increased 87%

Footnotes:

There are multiple contributing factors to these outcomes: PSSR sales reorganization, things outside our control, expense management, focus on "other income items," like shop supplies and fuel/mileage recovery and some windfalls associated with income taken through maintenance reserve accounts, etc.

However, unequivocally, I can state implementing the few key performance measures listed above and the associated structure and cultural changes has had the greatest impact on the improved business outcomes.

In terms of people questioning the timeline and expecting a faster return on investment, i.e. workshop hosted in 2010, Parts measures and practices put in place in 2011, Service measures and practices put in place in 2013. This was **our** timeline, based on **our** situation.

The outcomes are indisputable and directly tied to focus on the key areas I covered above. I would be happy to share in greater detail the many headwinds faced in implementing these changes faster.

Chris Shields, Vice President Product Support
Hugg and Hall Equipment Co.
chriss@hugghall.com

READER's GUIDE to *Achieving Excellence in Dealer/Distributor Performance*

The Master's Program in Dealer Management
Why This Book Set Is Essential To your Dealer Development Success

In the highly-acclaimed *Achieving Excellence* text, Walter begins by focusing today on how dealers can <u>immediately increase</u> profitability, cash flow, dealer market share and customer retention. **Build strengths today.**

Walter continues in *Strategies, Tactics, Operations* by providing in-depth insight on how dealers can build a <u>sustainable strategy</u> and structure their dealer organization to keep winning. **Ensure a better tomorrow.**

Walter examines the <u>Critical Profit Variables</u> essential for dealer success. He delineates and expands each performance metric with practical "how to" guidelines, case studies and, occasionally horror stories that could have been avoided. Practical programs to strengthen and increase profitability and market share in new machinery sales, rentals, used equipment, service and parts. Substantial sections are focused on Aftermarket Management and Machinery Sales Management with 65 charts, tables, forms and management tools.

Walter starts his 564 page text by building a Strategic Vision and providing a practical "how to" process for creating a winning product/market Strategy. His emphasis is on how to judiciously utilize scarce and costly resources. He examines Tactics for the proper utilization of the right resources at the right time. And, he defines the specifics of Operations Excellence in each Revenue Center through more than 650 <u>Best Practices</u> in new and used machinery, service, parts and rentals. What must you do well to gain and maintain competitive advantage? What execution skills are essential to your success?

Walt McDonald has assembled great insight and advice that he has learned over 40 years as a consultant and educator the industrial equipment industry. His continuously updated material is presented for all levels of management and for all aspects of the business.
Tim Hilton, Former CEO, Carolina Handling, Inc.
Executive Coach and Consultant

This is a one of a kind culmination of a lifetime's work. There is nothing else like it... a crowning achievement.
Jim Wilson, Retired Manager, Dealer Development, MCFA.
42 yrs. with Caterpillar Companies

Walter J. McDonald

The Master's Program in Dealer Management
What's In Book Three, the Essential
Dealer Problem-Solving Handbook?

McDonald's **Handbook** is a great guide to finding solutions to sales and operations problems.

Problem areas are listed by Revenue Center in the *Handbook*: New Equipment, Used Equipment, Rentals, Service and Parts plus a special section on Dealer Principal/ Ownership issues. Problems are presented followed by page number references in Books 1, 2 and 3.

A Coach's Corner gives each Revenue Center Manager fresh, new insight into the priority issues of that responsibility.

Industry Leader Comments:

These are the best books/tools for understanding the various departments in a dealership that I have ever seen.
Bill Rowan, CEO, Sunbelt Industrial Trucks

Walter McDonald has assembled great insight and advice that he has learned over 40 years as a consultant and educator in the industrial equipment industry. His continuously updated material is presented for all levels of management and for all aspects of the business.
Tim Hilton, Former CEO, Carolina Handling,

This is one-of-a-kind culmination of a lifetime's work. There is nothing else like it... a crowning achievement.
Jim Wilson, Retired Manager, Dealer Development, MCFA.
42 yrs. with Caterpillar.

TITLES are NOW AVAILABLE ON *AMAZON.COM*
or direct from mcdonaldgroupinc.com

The McDonald Group, Inc. ● *Walt@McDonaldGroupInc.com* ● www.McDonaldGroupInc.com
THE GLOBAL LEADER IN DEALER DEVELOPMENT

> ## The McDonald Group, Inc.
> ## Institute for Dealer Development
> *Master's Program in Dealer Management Workshop*
> Created and Presented by Walter J. McDonald, CMC,

- ☐ For Your Entire Dealer Management Team, All Locations: New and Used Machinery Sales, Rentals, Parts, Service and Finance

- ☐ Work Together to:
  - ✓ Strengthen Market Position, Expand Market Share
  - ✓ Improve Profitability, Return on Assets
  - ✓ Sharpen Teamwork, Build Problem-Solving Skills
  - ✓ Build Momentum Required for Annual Dealer Awards

Workshop Highlights...

- ☐ Work as a TEAM to Audit each Revenue Center's operations against our detailed high-performance dealer BEST PRACTICES checklist.

- ☐ Identify and discuss the critical success factors for each Revenue Center that contribute to enhanced cash flow, vigorous profitability, and improved market share as well as qualifications for Manufacturer Dealer Award Programs.

- ☐ Work as a TEAM to develop joint ACTION PLANS to improve sales, profitability and growth in each Revenue Center. Build performance improvement plans critical to your success.

> *The very best industry-specific workshop for Owners, General Managers, Department Managers and Financial Managers to help improve profitability, return on assets and cash flow, sharpen teamwork and build management problem-solving skills. We recommend the entire top management team participate, working together toward overall improvement in each revenue center.*

2½ -Day Workshop Agenda...

- **NEW MACHINERY BUSINESS MANAGEMENT.** Complete our 102-question best practices audit of your new machinery operations. Discuss market share and margin improvement strategies. Review how Team Selling gives competitive edge. Build account intelligence profiles. Examine best industry practices to improve deal visibility and profitable market share, achieving sales and profit performance benchmarks.

- **USED MACHINERY OPERATIONS.** Audit your used machinery operations. Examine the Seven AXIOMS for a highly profitable used equipment business. Discuss successful techniques for improving inventory turns, margins, used equipment appraisals and valuations.

- **RENTAL EQUIPMENT OPERATIONS.** Audit your rental equipment operations. Examine successful practices in equipment rental market assessment, revenue and profit control and, rental maintenance control techniques. Discuss rental trouble-shooting checklist and best rental practices.

- **SERVICE OPERATIONS.** Complete our 177-question service operations best practices audit. Learn how to improve productivity and profitability. Discuss how to reduce rework, improve field service technician productivity, and raise customer satisfaction levels. See how incremental service billings yield huge revenue gains. Examine field-proven aftermarket Service marketing and sales techniques. Examine how to reduce days in Work in Process (WIP).

- **PARTS OPERATIONS.** Conduct our 96-question parts operations best practices audit. Review how to significantly improve parts revenue and service levels. Learn how to avoid large cash traps. See how to calculate if the proposed discount is a "good deal." Discuss successful aftermarket Parts marketing and sales techniques. Examine how to eliminate dead stock, improve off-shelf fill rate, turns and margins. Learn how service and parts can better collaborate for mutual success and greatly improved customer satisfaction.

READER's GUIDE to *Achieving Excellence in Dealer/Distributor Performance*

- ☐ **CUSTOMER SERVICE & RETENTION.** Complete our best practices audit of your customer service operations. Learn how to structure a highly effective Customer Retention effort throughout the dealership. See results from The McDonald Group's studies on why customers leave. Examine how machinery customers define VALUE. Identify employee performance standards essential to Customer Retention. Build programs to improve "Value Delivery" in every customer interaction. Special free take-home employee training package.

- ☐ **TEAM SELLING AND COLLABORATION.** Learn how to establish Aftermarket Product Support as a barrier against competitors. Gain insight into what customers expect and how to best respond. Structure Product Support as a significant VALUE-ADDED factor in New, Used and Rental Equipment sales effort.

- ☐ **STRATEGIC ACTION PLANS FOR IMPROVEMENT.** Develop practical, written Management Action Plans to improve sales, profitability return on assets and positive cash in each Revenue Center. Project the Financial Impact and create practical steps to achieve your objectives.

- ☐ **MAJOR CLASS PROJECT Assignment.** Prepare and present a detailed profit improvement strategy to increase retail margins, improve return on assets and cash flow in your area of responsibility for your business. Resources include workshop materials and exercises plus numerous industry publications by The McDonald Group, Inc. Private coaching support for this important assignment will also be provided by your instructor.

Workshop Preparatory Exercises...

Participants complete a set of preparatory readings and diagnostic exercises, benchmarking 60 critical quantitative dealer performance areas. Reading assignments in *Achieving Excellence in Dealer/Distributor Performance* and *Strategies, Tactics, Operations for Achieving Dealer Excellence*.

- ☐ **SIX MONTH FORMAL REVIEW.** Participants and Instructor meet again; discuss progress; examine obstacles; refine attack strategy; move to next level.

The McDonald Group, Inc.
Institute for Dealer Development
Executive Sales Management Workshop
Executive Selling Skills Workshop
Created and Presented by Walter J. McDonald, CMC,

Dealer Executives, Sales Managers Attend All 4 Days

EXPERIENCED SALES PROFESSIONALS	NEWLY APPOINTED SALES PROFESSIONALS
☑ Update	☑ Essential Tools, Skills
☑ Renew	☑ Accelerated Start-Up
☑ Refresh	☑ Right Track Early
☑ Re-Challenge	☑ Find More New Deals
☑ Build on Strengths	☑ More Deals Closed

1½ -Day Private Session with Dealer Principals and Sales Managers...

- ❐ **MARKET SHARE AND PROFIT IMPROVEMENT STRATEGY.** Special strategic project assignment to quickly build more profitable equipment business.

- ❐ **HIGH PROBABILITY RECRUITING.** How the real world of "tough-minded" sales management model can improve your odds of recruiting success. Identify "high probability" success characteristics. Use the "Job Difficulty Chart" to assess the experience history of your candidate.

- ❐ **ACCELERATED START-UP.** Create an "Accelerated Start-up Plan" for the new or "renewed" field sales rep. Define what must be accomplished in the first 30, 60 and 90 days. Guide your new recruit through the essential job orientation, product and applications knowledge, selling skills practice, key account introductions, sales tools organization and territory planning essential to a quick, highly successful start-up.

READER's GUIDE to *Achieving Excellence in Dealer/Distributor Performance*

- ☐ **LARGE ACCOUNT DEVELOPMENT.** Create a key account penetration plan. Examine highly effective key account profiling techniques. Learn what *value points* are most critical to your customers. Identify how your dealership can build important linkages and establish solid relationships, identify key influencers and decision makers.

- ☐ **PERFORMANCE IMPROVEMENT.** See if you have a training problem or a motivation problem. Evaluate each rep on critical performance essential to achieving high sales rep performance in deal visibility and deal closure rates. Prepare a performance development program for each of your sales reps.

- ☐ **TRAINING and DEVELOPMENT.** Audit your own Sales Management coaching performance. Identify which five coaching practices contribute most to improved performance. Discuss the most effective ways to teach and coach your sales reps to high levels of individual success.

- ☐ **MAJOR CLASS PROJECTS.** Create an Accelerated "Quick Start" Program for new or "renewed" sales reps. Coaching will be available from the Instructor for this important assignment. Develop a formal performance improvement plan for each of your existing sales professionals.

- ☐ **PERSONAL ACTION PLANS.** Document your personal Action Plans for success. Create and present a formal sales operations improvement plan for your dealership. Personal coaching from the Instructor on this individual project.

Sales Manager Workshop Preparatory Exercises...

Participants complete a set of preparatory readings and exercises. You will benchmark key performances for each of your sales reps as a pre-workshop diagnostic performance review. Short management reading assignments.

- ☐ **SIX MONTH FORMAL REVIEW.** Participants and Instructor meet again; discuss progress; examine obstacles; refine attack strategy; move to next level.

Walter J. McDonald

The McDonald Group, Inc.
Executive Selling Skills Workshop
2½ -Day Session with Managers and Sales Reps...

> **HIGHLIGHTS:** Audit your entire equipment and aftermarket sales operations. Study and discuss what "really works" in dealer sales today. Improve "deal visibility" and "deale closure rate" skills. Learn account development strategies to identify and penetrate high margin accounts and prospects. Master the "sales diagnostic questioning" process and techniques in customized sales presentations and case studies. See how to avoid the most common sales mistakes. Create an Action Plan to run the territory like a highly successful business.

- ❏ **TOOLS and KNOWLEDGE.** Sales Tools Operations Audit. How to create and maintain a "winning edge." How to achieve a mental fitness level essential to success. Mental exercises that contribute most to mental fitness. How to build expertise in the nine critical sales skill areas.

- ❏ **SALES PROSPECTING.** Sales Prospecting Operations Audit. Identify ALL of the sales prospecting technology tools available today. Study how market segmentation tools can greatly improve prospecting success. Evaluate how well you are utilizing each prospecting technology. Learn how to overcome obstacles to prospecting. How to identify the premiere prospect. How to maximize your deal awareness.

- ❏ **RELATIONSHIP and TRUST.** Relationship Building Operations Audit. How to move up the Relationship Hierarchy. How to qualify the prospect. How to best utilize the sales cycle. How to remove the greatest obstacles to sales success. How to structure an entry strategy, influence choice and create differentiation. How to probe, question and listen. How to determine strength of incumbent competitor. What

Executive Selling Skills Workshop (cont.)

diagnostic questions enable you to deliver real value? How to build trust and credibility. How to read customer psychology and body language clues to sell them the way they want to be sold. How to greatly improve your deal closure rate.

- ☐ TIME and TERRITORY MANAGEMENT. Time and Territory Management Operations Audit. How to structure, organize and implement a dynamite account coverage plan. How to improve "return on energy." How to plan for and maintain the necessary sales activity level essential to success. What selling skills improve new account prospecting and deal "Visibility." How to shorten the sales development cycle. Territory strategies that pay quick dividends. How to allocate time between prospecting, selling, administration and investment/training to optimize territory effectiveness.

- ☐ PRESENTATIONS and DEMONSTRATIONS. Presentations and Demonstrations Audit. How to become a "problem detective." Learn to ask questions that give you control. Examine the kinds of questions too often asked by rookies. Determine best approaches for each prospect. Learn the rules of power presentations and how to uncover hot buttons. How to confirm customer recognition and acceptance of "value points."

Special customized case studies for your dealership's types of sales opportunities. Sales teams prepare a walk-around "features-functions-benefits" sales presentation based on the problem-solving selling model. Demonstration challenges are based on assigned tailored case studies built around realistic prospects in your markets with your products against your local competitors.

More...

Executive Selling Skills Workshop (cont.)

- ☐ **NEGOTIATING, HANDLING OBJECTIONS and THE CLOSE.** Evaluate how you are currently handling objections and advancing the deal. What skills contribute most to improved "closure rate." How to overcome customer skepticism and gain commitment. How objections contribute to sales success. How to eliminate most objections through better diagnostic questions. Why you should make it easy for the prospect to object. How to "de-fuse" objections early in the sales process. How to test your vulnerability in the deal. How to recognize buying signals. How to identify and overcome prospect FEARS. How and when to negotiate. How to apply eight alternate closing techniques in your territory.

- ☐ **COMMON SALES MISTAKES vs. HIGHLY SUCCESSFUL SALES HABITS.** What do the very best equipment and aftermarket sales professionals do and not do. What insights can you take back home for your territory.

- ☐ **PERSONAL ACTION PLANS.** Each participant will develop and present a set of practical, personal Action Plans to improve sales effectiveness and achieve sales and financial targets in his/her area of responsibility. Follow-up coaching assistance from the Instructor will help ensure that the Action Plans are practical and provide measurable results.

Sales Professional Workshop Preparatory Exercises...

In order to get the most out of the program, sales reps are asked to complete a set of short preparatory readings and exercises before the session.

- ☐ **SIX MONTH FORMAL REVIEW.** Participants and Instructor meet again; discuss progress; examine obstacles; refine attack strategy; move to next level.

READER's GUIDE to *Achieving Excellence in Dealer/Distributor Performance*

ABOUT THE AUTHOR

Walter McDonald is founder of The McDonald Group, Inc., a private consulting firm focusing on marketing and business strategies, executive education and development. For the past four decades, Walter has been a highly respected industry consultant and management seminar leader. He has worked on business consulting assignments assisting manufacturers and dealers improve operations, market share, profitability and customer retention.

Walter has written more than 50 articles in *Construction Equipment Distribution* and the *MHEDA Journal*. In 2017 Walter began publication of his internationally acclaimed six book series on Equipment Dealer Management and Development beginning with *Achieving Excellence in Dealer/Distributor Performance*. The complete set is known as *The Master's Program in Dealer Management*.

Walter is a popular guest speaker and specializes in customized in-company training programs. Walter has conducted well over 2,650 dealer management workshops throughout North America, Europe, the Far East and Australia. Dear Development clients include Caterpillar, Komatsu, Deere, Bobcat, Volvo CE, Vermeer, Ditch Witch, Case, JCB, Link Belt, Ingersoll-Rand, Astec Underground, Trimble, Hyster, Yale, Nissan Unicarriers, Toyota, Mitsubishi Caterpillar Forklift America, Raymond, Crown, Kelley Dock Systems, Cummins, Detroit Diesel, Volvo Trucks, Kenworth, Peterbilt, MACK, Freightliner, Thermo King, Kohler, Emergency One Fire Trucks, Pierce Fire Trucks, AED and MHEDA.

Prior to his management consulting career, Walter held several sales, marketing and general management positions at the senior level including Vice President and General Manager of a $160 million distribution company. Walter received his Management Consultant Certification (CMC) from the Institute of Management Consultants. He graduated *Cum Laude* from Louisiana State University with a B.A. in Economics, attended M.I.T.'s Sloan School of Management and pursued graduate studies in marketing and finance at the University of Chicago's Graduate School of Business.

His web site is www.mcdonaldgroupinc.com. Walter would be happy to discuss any of his work with you at *Walt@McDonaldGroupInc.com*.

Walter J. McDonald

Free White Papers Available
on www.mcdonaldgroupinc.com

Hierarchy of Dealer Knowledge: On Becoming a More Effective Dealer Manager

21 Gorilla Marketing Ideas for Equipment Dealers

Accelerated Start-up: How to Get Your Brand New Sales Rep Productive in Less than 100 days

How to Sell Engineered Systems

Photo Shoot on the African Serengeti

Sales Rep Confidential: Are You a Dinosaur?

Successful Technician Recruiting: 10 Field-Proven Techniques that Work

Product Support: a Barrier to Competition

16 Tools to Build Your Service Labor Business

Product Support as a Competitive Weapon

Four Dimensions of Dealer Development

Four Dealer Profit Improvement Strategies

How to Optimize Business Value –
Succession Planning: Twists and Turns

How to Avoid Problems with OEM Agreements – Are they Functional or Fractured?

www.ingramcontent.com/pod-product-compliance
Lightning Source LLC
Chambersburg PA
CBHW062231220526
45471CB00009B/3439